IN FOCUS: NATIVE AMERICANS

SIOUX

HISTORY AND CULTURE

MARK STEWART

Published in 2026 by Cavendish Square Publishing, LLC
2544 Clinton Street, Buffalo, NY 14224

Website: cavendishsq.com

Portions of this work were originally authored by Lorraine Harrison and published as *Sioux* (Spotlight on Native Americans). All new material this edition authored by Mark Stewart.

Publisher: Katie Kawa
Book Design: Lisa Miley

Portions of this work were reviewed by: Robert J. Conley, Former Sequoyah Distinguished Professor at Western Carolina University and Director of Native American Studies at Morningside College and Montana State University.

Photo Credits: Wollertz/Shutterstock.com (4); Marilyn Angel Wynn/Nativestock/Getty Images (5, 7); George Catlin/Smithsonian American Art Museum (6 top*); Seth Eastman/National Gallery of Art (6 bottom*); Michael Nowack/Harper's Weekly (9*); R.L. Kelly (10*); Library of Congress (11*, 12*, 13 top*, 18*, 24*); Frank Leslie's Illustrated Newspaper (13 bottom*); Carlisle Indian School Digital Resource Center (15*); Heyn Photo (16*); Metropolitan Museum of Art (17*); Author Unknown (19*); John Coletti/Photolibrary/Getty Images (20); J.A. Anderson/ Library of Congress (21*); Ted Hall (22); John Sunderland/Denver Post/Getty Images (23 top); National Park Service (23 bottom); AFP/ AFP/Getty Images (25); Robert Van Der Hilst/Gamma-Rapho/Getty Images (26); J. Borden/National Park Service (27); Wolfgang Kaehler/ LightRocket via Getty Images (28); Hyoung Chang/Denver Post/Getty Images (29).

Cover images (clockwise from top): Seth Eastman/National Gallery of Art*; Wolfgang Kaehler/LightRocket via Getty Images (28); Library of Congress*; Library of Congress* (image includes Northern Arapaho leaders); Herman Heyn/Library of Congress*; Edward Curtis/Library of Congress*.

*These images are in the public domain.

Cataloging-in-Publication Data
Names: Stewart, Mark, 1960 July 7-.
Title: Sioux history and culture / Mark Stewart.
Description: Buffalo, NY : Cavendish Square Publishing, 2026. | Series: In focus: Native Americans | Includes glossary and index.
Identifiers: ISBN 9781502674852 (pbk.) | ISBN 9781502674869 (library bound) | ISBN 9781502674876 (ebook)
Subjects: LCSH: Dakota Indians--Juvenile literature. | Lakota Indians--Juvenile literature. | Sioux Nation--History--Juvenile literature. | Indians of North America--Juvenile literature. | Indigenous peoples--Social life and customs--Juvenile literature.
Classification: LCC E99.D1 S94 2026 | DDC 978.004'975243--dc23

CPSIA compliance information: Batch #CS26CSQ: For further information contact Cavendish Square Publishing LLC at 1-877-980-4450.
Printed in the United States of America

CONTENTS

ABOUT OUR GLOSSARY

In this book, there may be several words or terms you are reading for the first time, or words that are familiar but used in an unusual way. All of these words appear in **bold type** throughout the book and are defined on page 30.

I AM THE LAND

The Black Hills of South Dakota and Wyoming are among the most diverse and abundant **ecosystems** in North America. The region is located on the western edge of the Great Plains and is marked by rugged mountains, lush grasslands, and picturesque valleys. The dense evergreen forests that hug the slopes give the Black Hills their dark appearance from far away. Humans have called this part of the continent home for more than 12,000 years.

About 250 years ago, most of the Dakota, Lakota, and Nakota people—known collectively as the Sioux—

Medicine men and women provide an important link between the Dakota, Lakota, and Nakota people and their environment.

moved west along the Missouri River into the Black Hills. They traveled from lands near Lake Superior, where they had lived for more than 500 years. Generations of conflict with the Ojibwa people (also known as the Ojibwe or Chippewa) forced them to move from the Great Lakes region. Before that, scholars believe that the Sioux culture had developed to the south, in the Mississippi Valley.

As the Sioux moved west, they adopted more of a Plains culture. They became skilled horsemen and hunters of bison, relying less and less on their traditions of farming, fishing, foraging, and hunting woodland creatures. Their migration into parts of current-day

The Black Hills have been inhabited by humans for thousands of years.

▲ The Sioux were skilled hunters of Great Plains bison.

Nebraska, South Dakota, Montana, and Wyoming brought them into conflict with other tribes. In some cases, they made alliances. In others, they fought for their survival. By the time the Lakota Sioux settled in the Black Hills, they had pushed the Crow and Cheyenne people off the land.

During this time, the Sioux had limited contact with Europeans. They did business with French and English fur traders, but it was never a crucial part of their economy. By constantly pushing west, they avoided many of the diseases that devasted cultures to the south and east. The Sioux acquired their horses from neighboring tribes, who had acquired them from Spanish settlers in the late 1600s and early 1700s. The Lakota Sioux, in particular, adapted their hunting, fighting, and raiding skills to the horse.

As was the case with many Native American tribes, the Sioux did not choose the name by which the world came to know them. The root of this word is *nadouwesou*, or "little snakes," from the language of their enemies, the Ojibwes. It was not meant to be a compliment—and many tribe members now favor identifying themselves with other words. French traders shortened *nadouwesou* to *sioux*. The Sioux referred to themselves as *oceti sakowi*—or "Seven Council Fires"—as well as Dakota, Lakota, or Nakota, which identified them by the **dialects** that they spoke.

Today, the seven major bands within the Sioux Nation are the Oglala, Brule, Minneconjou, Sans Arc, Two Kettle, Blackfoot, and Hunkpapa.

◀ This 1851 painting shows tribe members playing a stickball game with the Black Hills in the background.

FIRST CONTACT

Starting in the mid-1800s, American settlers arrived on Sioux lands in ever-increasing numbers. Some were headed farther west along the Oregon Trail, but many planned on staying. The United States government established military bases to protect the settlers and made treaties in an attempt to keep the peace. A long drought reduced the bison herds on which the Sioux depended for food, and white settlers killed the animals in large numbers, too. Soon the Sioux people, many of whom were on the edge of starvation, began fighting back.

In 1854, a misunderstanding over a stray cow exploded into violence, and a **detachment** of soldiers sent to a Sioux encampment from Fort Laramie in Wyoming was wiped out. This began more than 20 years of on-and-off fighting between different Sioux groups and the U.S. military.

The hanging of 38 Santee warriors in 1862 was America's largest mass execution.

One of these groups, the Santee Sioux, had moved back to Minnesota as part of a treaty that promised them annual payments. When the government broke that promise, they attacked a nearby village in 1862 and killed hundreds of farming families. Thirty-eight warriors were later hanged in the nation's largest mass execution.

I AM A WARRIOR

The Sioux warrior tradition was part of every young boy's life, often before he took his first steps. His mother's lullabies celebrated success in hunting and war, while his father's stories spoke of the importance of honor, skill, and courage. Above all, Sioux warriors were expected to be defenders of their people.

The Lakota, Dakota, and Nakota groups occupied a wide range of landscapes and ecosystems. Understanding the environment was important for hunting and crucial for battle. Whether on foot or horseback, Sioux warriors knew how to

◀ This photo of Spotted Eagle shows a Sioux war club.

Red Cloud, a famous Lakota warrior, led his people to victory over U.S. forces in several battles during the 1860s.

make the most of the local terrain and which weapons would be most effective. They could shoot quickly and accurately while riding—either with bows and arrows or firearms—and used **lances** in close combat. In hand-to-hand fighting, they used knives and clubs with great skill and effectiveness.

While some Native groups valued bravery in warfare at all costs, Sioux warriors were taught to be strategic and cunning. Killing or wounding an enemy without **sustaining** an injury yourself was looked upon as a great triumph. Sioux war chiefs were particularly adept at coordinating large-scale attacks, **flanking** their enemies, and keeping them guessing at all times. Warriors had great confidence in their leaders, which helped them stay calm and organized.

Two of the most **revered** Sioux war leaders were Sitting Bull and Crazy Horse. In 1876, they led groups of Lakota and Northern Cheyenne warriors in a fight against U.S. government forces after gold was discovered in the Black Hills. This was sacred territory, and the Sioux were determined to defend it with their lives. They scored a victory over the United States Army at the Battle of Rosebud on June 17th in Montana Territory. Nine days later, Lieutenant General George Custer launched an attack on a large village at the Little Big Horn River and was badly defeated by the Lakotas and their Northern Cheyenne and Arapaho allies.

▲ Chief Sitting Bull was a feared opponent of the U.S. Army during the 1860s and 1870s.

The victories over the U.S. Army in the spring of 1876 were followed by a series of defeats. In early 1877, the conflict known as the Sioux Wars came to an end. Sitting Bull fled to Canada with his people, but returned to the U.S. in 1881 and surrendered in return for **amnesty** for his people.

◀ This painting shows Sioux horsemen during the Battle of Little Bighorn in 1876.

A NEW REALITY

Agreements between the United States government and different groups of Lakota, Dakota, and Nakota people began in the 1850s. However, bloody skirmishes and outright warfare continued during the 1860s. Following the American Civil War, the government set its sights on making it safe for Americans to journey west. That meant dealing with the Sioux and other western tribes—either through compromise or brute force.

In 1868, a treaty was signed that created the Great Sioux Reservation. It recognized the sacred Black Hills as part of a protected homeland. Six years later, gold was discovered in the Black Hills and prospectors flooded into Sioux territory and occupied their hunting grounds. The miners demanded protection from the government, which ignited a new period of conflict. In 1877, the Sioux were forced to give up much of their land in the Black Hills and move onto smaller reservations. Ownership of this land is still under dispute a century-and-a-half later.

Four Sioux boys pose for a photo after arriving at the Carlisle Indian Industrial School in 1879.

The reservation system was designed to force Native Americans, including the Sioux, to abandon their traditions, religions, and languages. Starting in 1879, dozens of Sioux children were sent to the Carlisle Indian Industrial School in Pennsylvania. Its goal was to **assimilate** them into mainstream American society, which meant white society. Many died there. Efforts to return their remains to tribal lands continue to this day.

BEING SIOUX

Like all Great Plains people, the Sioux relied on bison herds for food, clothing, and shelter. Every part of the animals was put to use. They fashioned bison horns into spoons and other utensils and made weapons from their larger bones. The hunting skills they developed as a Woodlands culture were not ideal for hunting bison on foot, but once the Sioux acquired horses, they became more mobile and enjoyed an almost unlimited amount of food. This enabled their population to grow quickly. In a generation or two, they became the dominant group along much of the Missouri River.

In times when bison were less plentiful, Sioux hunters relied on other large mammals for food and skins, including deer, elk, and wild sheep. They also harvested herbs, berries, and wild turnips, and tapped

◀ A man identified as John Comes Again poses in traditional Lakota clothing.

A young Sioux boy poses with older members of his tribe.

maple trees for sugar. The Sioux grew crops such as corn, beans, and squash when and where they we able—and traded for them, too. However, they relied almost entirely on hunting and gathering for their food.

In Lakota, Dakota, and Nakota tradition, "wealth" was measured by the size and strength of the extended family, which included blood relatives and members of the same **clan**. The Lakota word for this structure is *tiyospaye*. It served as a bond of trust and support, as well as a form of leadership. In a Sioux village, families that formed a tiyospaye typically lived side-by-side in a large circle, which symbolized this spirit of harmony.

The leader of a tiyospaye was chosen for his wisdom, courage, and **compassion**, as well as his ability

to gain spiritual guidance from dreams and visions. The most respected leaders were called *nacas*. They formed a tribal council called the *Naca Omincia*, which had the power to make decisions of national importance for the Sioux. Village chiefs were adult males, while both women and men served as healers who could cure illnesses and tend to spiritual needs.

◀ A Sioux woman named Susan Frost poses in traditional clothing in this 1899 photograph.

The role of women in Sioux society focused on preparing food and medicine, tending to household matters, and making clothing from bison, elk, or deer hides. Men wore full-length leggings, while women wore knee-length dresses and leggings that reached to their knees. Moccasins and clothing that included colorful beadwork were usually reserved for special occasions.

During the tribe's time in the Great Lakes region, families lived in wigwams made from bent **saplings** covered in bark. They lived in tipis (also spelled tepees) after moving to the Great Plains. In both cases, responsibility for building and decorating these structures fell to women.

The only woman recognized as a chief among the Sioux was known as Eagle Woman That All Look At, or Eagle Woman for short. She was married twice, each time to a powerful fur trader, which elevated her status among white settlers and her own people. Eagle Woman was an **advocate** for peace, often putting herself in great peril during the many conflicts of the 1860s and 1870s. In 1882, Eagle Woman became the first Native American woman to sign a treaty with the U.S. government.

SOMETHING SACRED

Like most Native American tribes, the Lakota, Dakota, and Nakota believe in a Creator, *Wankan Tanka*, which they also call the Great Spirit or Great Mystery. They believe it is present in all things, including rocks, trees, animals, water, and wind. They seek guidance from *Wankan Tanka* in their dreams and visions.

For more than two centuries, Bear Butte in the Black Hills has been a place for fasting and praying as part of a **vision quest** (*hanblecha*). The Sioux believe it is a sacred bear that watches the Great Plains. In 1961, Bear Butte became a state park, which limited access to tribal members. Use of the site is still in dispute.

The Lakota, Dakota, and Nakota people performed many of their spiritual ceremonies in a dance house like this one.

Among the many spiritual practices that promote harmony and connect the Sioux people to the Great Spirit is the Sun Dance (*wiwankawacipi*), which is held every summer. It helps to cleanse the spirit and renews the promise to work for the good of the community. Other important ceremonies include the Sweat Lodge (*inipi*) and the sharing of the Sacred Pipe (*canupa*), which is filled with a mixture herbs, berries, roots, bark, and tobacco.

These are three of the Seven Sacred Ceremonies, which play an important role in connecting the people to their history and traditions. Another way this is

◀ Bear Butte has been sacred ground for the Sioux for more than two centuries.

▲
Mona Susan Power discourages the continued use of the term "Sioux."

accomplished is through the creative work of artists and writers. Mona Susan Power, who grew up in Chicago, Illinois, is a celebrated author of novels, short stories, and essays—and a descendant of Dakota chiefs and influential female leaders.

"When I was a little girl, teachers in school told me that I came from a group of people who did not respect women or choose them as leaders," she recalls. "When I tried to share my own family experience, I was told to be quiet. This is why I became a writer—to share my truth with the world."

Power has used her popularity to discourage the use of the word Sioux, which is viewed by some as a **derogatory** term.

"While my people accepted the term of Sioux placed upon us by others for many years, we've now gone back to using our original names for our tribe and

bands," she explains. "So I'm actually *Iháŋkthuŋwaŋna Dakhóta*, and not Sioux."

Power has followed in the footsteps of other well-known creative people who embraced a commitment to **activism**, including Vine Deloria Jr. and Floyd Red Crow Westerman. Deloria, an author and educator who grew up on the Standing Rock Reservation in South Dakota, brought national attention to Native American issues in the 1960s and 1970s. Westerman, who was born on the Lake Traverse Reservation (also in South Dakota), was a popular musician and actor who became an outspoken advocate for Indigenous cultural preservation.

▲ The books written by Vine Deloria Jr. brought attention to Native American issues in the 1960s and 1970s.

Although the Lakota, Dakota, and Nakota people did not journey west until the 1700s, the Black Hills play an important role in their creation story. According to tribal elders, the first Sioux came from Star Nation to a place beneath the earth. Then, they emerged from Wind Cave in the Black Hills. They call the Black Hills *Paha Sapa*, which means "the heart of everything that is."

PAST, PRESENT, FUTURE

The **transition** to reservation life was hard on the Sioux people. Sadness and frustration led them to embrace the Ghost Dance religion, which promised the return of bison herds, **reanimation** of their deceased loved ones, and the disappearance of the white man. Fearing the start of another war, a Sioux leader named Big Foot attempted to make peace in 1890. The army was unaware of his peaceful intentions and attacked his band at Wounded Knee Creek in South Dakota. More than 250 men, women, and children were killed.

The Ghost Dance was viewed as a threat by the U.S. government in the late 1800s.

Today, the Sioux Nation includes 12 federally recognized groups. Federal recognition means that tribal government can communicate directly with the U.S. government. There is one in Nebraska, three in Minnesota, seven in South Dakota, and one (the Standing Rock Sioux Tribe) whose reservation includes parts of North and South Dakota. Approximately 160,000 people identify themselves as Sioux, with roughly half living on tribal lands. Unemployment and poverty are worse on some reservations than others, but rates are significantly higher than in the overall U.S. population.

In 1973, Wounded Knee was in the news again. About 200 Oglala Sioux and other activists from the American Indian Movement (AIM) occupied the town, which is now part of the Pine Ridge Indian Reservation. They hoped to force the United States government to reopen treaty negotiations and treat Native Americans more fairly. Two of their leaders were shot and killed during the 71-day standoff with the FBI and U.S. Marshals. The protest attracted global attention to the long-standing problems faced on reservations and energized Native Americans to advocate for their rights.

The Pipestone National Monument in southwestern Minnesota—considered sacred ground by the Sioux—draws more than 70,000 visitors every year.

Reservation economies differ, but all of them strive to develop and manage their natural resources. Ranching and farming, tourism (including casinos), and government jobs provide much of the employment and income. To further develop economic opportunities, tribal representatives work with the U.S. government to improve health and education, and to overcome problems of isolation. Many people live on reservations that are 100 miles (161 km) or more from the nearest airport, and must leave their lands to buy some of their basic needs.

◀ A Lakota woman poses with her horse. Horses remain an important part of Sioux tradition and culture.

A tribe member speaks during an event held at a memorial to the Sioux warriors who fought at the battle of Little Big Horn.

With support from the government that has taken so much from them for so long, the Sioux now operate programs aimed at strengthening the connection between tribal members and their history and culture, while also developing businesses that embrace the idea of *wikozani*: the Dakota word for health, well-being, and community values.

◀ A young Sioux girl participates in a powwow in Washington State. The Sioux celebrate their heritage and culture at events around the country.

GLOSSARY AND FURTHER READING

GLOSSARY

Activism—The effort to encourage social change.

Advocate—Someone who supports a cause.

Amnesty—Official forgiveness for breaking a rule or law.

Assimilate—Become absorbed into a new culture.

Clan—A close-knit extended family related by kinship or common ancestors.

Compassion—Sympathy for the suffering of others.

Derogatory—Disrespectful and hurtful.

Detachment—A group of soldiers sent on a mission.

Dialects—Slightly different forms of a language.

Ecosystems—Group of living and nonliving things that create nutrients and energy within various areas.

Flanking—Maneuvering around the sides of an enemy.

Lances—Spear-like weapons used by mounted warriors.

Reanimation—Bringing something back to life.

Revered—Deeply respected and admired.

Saplings—Young, flexible trees.

Sustaining—Suffering something unpleasant, including a wound or injury.

Transition—The process of changing from one condition to another.

Vision Quest—A spiritual journey experienced by young men in many western Native American tribes.

BOOKS

Krupat, Arnold. *Boarding School Voices: Carlisle Indian School Students Speak*. Lincoln, NE: University of Nebraska Press, 2021.

Rossiter, Brienna. *The Trail of Tears*. Mendota Heights, MN: North Star Editions, 2025.

Tyler, Ron. *Native Americans: The Complete Plates of McKenney, Catlin, and Bodmer*. Cologne, Germany: Taschen America, 2024.

Various Authors. *My Life: Growing Up Native in America*. New York, NY: MTV Books/Simon & Schuster Children's Publishing, 2024.

ABOUT THE AUTHOR

MARK STEWART has written more than 150 non-fiction books for educational publishers, covering history, sports, and popular culture. His family tree tells a complex story common to many Americans. Mark's ancestors include some of the first European colonists, as well as the Indigenous people with whom early settlers interacted. Some faced off on the field of battle while others fought side-by-side. His 10th great-grandfather was **Myles Standish**, an officer on the ***Mayflower***, while his ninth great-grandmother was **Singing Bird Corbison**, who was described as a "Shawnee woman" but who was probably from the **Wampanoag** tribe. The Wampanoag people saved Standish and his fellow **Pilgrims** from starvation during the winter of 1620–21, forming the basis for the story of Thanksgiving. The descendants of Corbison and Standish blended into a single family in 1789, and then headed west in search of opportunity. This brought Mark's ancestors into direct conflict with Native people along the frontier in the 1700s and 1800s. Mark's sixth great-grandmother recalled frantically casting bullets for her husband as they defended their small Kentucky fort from an attack. Another served under 23-year-old **Abraham Lincoln** in the Illinois Militia during the Black Hawk War of 1832. Mark's more recent ancestors chose to fight their battles with words—as writers and editors of books, newspapers and magazines. In 2007, he authored a history of the **Indian Removal Act of 1830** and the infamous **Trail of Tears**.

INDEX

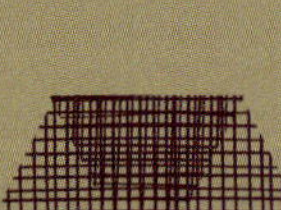